IAN GOUGE

FIRST-TIME VISIONS OF EARTH FROM SPACE

First published in paperback format by
Coverstory books, 2019

ISBN 978-1-9997840-7-2

Copyright © Ian Gouge 2019

The right of Ian Gouge to be identified as
the author of this work has been asserted by
them in accordance with the Copyright,
Designs and Patents Act 1988.

All characters and events in this publication.
other than those clearly in the public
domain, are fictitious and any resemblance
to real persons, living or dead, is purely
coincidental.

For details on the cover image, please see
the Acknowledgements section.

All rights reserved.

No part of this publication may be
reproduced, circulated, stored in a system
from which it can be retrieved, or
transmitted in any form without the prior
permission in writing of the publisher.

www.iangouge.com

www.coverstorybooks.com

FIRST-TIME VISIONS OF EARTH FROM SPACE

Other Books by Ian Gouge

Novels and Novellas

An Infinity of Mirrors - Coverstory books, 2018

Losing Moby Dick and Other Stories - Coverstory books, 2017

Losing Moby Dick - Kindle 2015

Writing to Gisella - Kindle 2015

Riding the Escalators - Kindle 2015

The Big Frog Theory - Coverstory books, 2018 (2nd. Ed.); Kindle, 2012

Short Stories

Degrees of Separation - Coverstory books, 2018

Secrets & Wisdom - Coverstory books, 2017

Poetry

After the Rehearsals - Coverstory books, 2018

Punctuations from History - Coverstory books, 2018

Human Archaeology - Paperback, 2017

Collected Poems (1979-2016) - Paperback, 2017

Caught off-guard, he still dreams aloud.

Contents

Introduction 9

Firsts

First-time Visions of Earth from Space 13
Cryptic 14
The Unwrapped Present 15
Experiments with Words 16
Approaching the Border 17
Cubism & Picasso 18
Diagnosis 19

Lasts

A Cracked Voice 23
Passion 24
Waves are not water 25
When floating turned to drowning 26
Anthropology 27
The Cut-out 28
The Irresistible Fall 29
Gladys 30
Congregation at a Twitcher's Sunset 32
Early Edition 33
Inheritance 35
Changing Trains 36
Did we know those days were golden? 38

And Somewhere in Between

Rumours of a breakthrough in the search for the meaning of life . 41
Harvesting 42
Gas Street Basin 43
Deauville 44
On the verge of new love 46
Attachment 47
Modern Warfare 48
20/20 49

ex-Curricula	50
Ganglands = Politics	51
Threat	52
DNA	53
Reconstruction	55
Undercurrent	56
The Mirage of Progress	57
Global Warning	58
Peasant Farming	59
The Hopeless Wager	60
Telling the time	61
The Thief	62
untitled haiku	63
The Myth of You	64
Fossil-hunting	65

※

Acknowledgements	67

Introduction

Having seen photographs taken on some of the first manned space flights and then read how Apollo astronauts struggled to describe what they had witnessed through the window of their spacecraft, I found myself fascinated by the difficulty they encountered. Not just the challenge of language and its casual inadequacy as a tool for expression - but also the astronauts' compulsive need to depict and interpret at all. The wonderful and totally 'authentic' images they captured (and which they would not see developed until after their flight, of course) were never going to be enough.

This impulse - and the poem it spawned - set a tone of sorts, and I began to write, hone, curate a few other poems that loosely fit the same theme. Initially these concentrated on either the nature of 'firsts' or the way we in which commit ourselves to the struggle to articulate. Later, I found my poems had begun to branch out and explore in their own way. A number of them were skating on the thin ice of 'lasts', and the question of what happens to us once we have the age - or wisdom - to be able to look back. This retrospection is, of course, a natural by-product of our journey through life, and I began to tease at whether our experience of looking in the rear view mirror - or into an ever-diminishing future - was not unlike those astronauts peering through a small porthole across the vacuum of space and trying to describe what they saw.

And there's the rub. At the heart of this collection - and of any such endeavour, be it poetry or prose - is an attempt to relay something; to lay it out, understand and interpret it, to wrestle with the brilliance and vagaries of language, and always, *in each and every instance*, to do so afresh. Every blank page is a first, like the raw film on which those negatives of the Earth were captured; every white space offers, in its own way, a similar journey of exploration; and in every instance, we are staring through a metaphorical porthole which can only provide an inadequate and restricted view of the whole. Most of our literary discoveries may be nebulous, but surely what they all strive to achieve is a meaningful interpretation of their subject and a perfection in execution which is ultimately out of reach, inevitably just beyond the periphery of our abilities - perhaps like an image part-glimpsed through a spaceship window and then lost forever.

No matter how hard we try, we never can "describe blue".

Ian Gouge, 2018

Firsts

First-time Visions of Earth from Space

Sailing in an endless star-studded sea
they tried to find words to convey reality.

Knowing a single image can never be all the story,
they are subject to an irrepressible desire
to record their glimpse of this improbable oasis.

Constrained by meaning and connotation
words are fault-full when searching for ways to describe blue.

Cryptic

Green. Round. Spiky.
On the black roughness of a pavement inappropriately made
the first horse-chestnut of the year.

Unexpected
it lays there like a gift

                or a promise;

a sentinel
vanguard of the future
prepared to sacrifice itself
to a misunderstanding boot,
a sacrifice made worthy
only if its message gets through.

The Unwrapped Present

Is it with care or with caution we unwrap it,
teasing at a knot of ribbon elaborately curled,
the see-through tape impeccably applied?

Seeking snags at corners, a naked edge,
we attempt to lift a seal, to break a bond,
to preserve the wrapping whole, unblemished.

We fail - once, twice - and in the end
discard this superficial skin as detritus,
crumpled and torn, the ribbon twisted,
the now-opaque tape finger-printed with us.

Liberated, it lies unopen on the table,
pristine edged, crease-free, perfect;
a universe of promise condensed into
a familiar house style, its title, name
proudly embossed as if rising to a challenge set.
Breathless on the edge of discovery
we ease back the cover, and read.

Experiments with Words

"We initially found them hopping around in a lab,
homely & ungainly & quite ordinary,
behaviours written into genes like automatons
- though that may not be the perfect analogy.

"Later, we set them free, trying
to get a clear picture of their wanderings,
giving them no choice but to travel
- both the escaping and then the coming back.
Being able to experiment like this
simply underscores how far we've come!"

Striving to be first to decipher a jumble of datasets,
we explore output in unprecedented detail
stressing ourselves over lattes and amaretti
and creating complex algorithms for calculators
- a nail-biter because the battery was failing.

Approaching the Border

Darkness' cover fails to muffle the sound
of heavy boots crunching arid rain-starved soil.
Impossible to see, ears become eyes
as we listen for tell-tale signs we are close.
One leaf like the next, touch is peripheral, and thirst
- not having taken water for days -
plays tricks with starved ambition.
Or perhaps it is the confusion of altitude;
if only we knew how high we had climbed!
Before darkness fell, the cloud-mist ahead
hung like a promise or a threat.
'It cannot be far', I say to myself,
forcing weary left-right repetition
as if it were mantra to a god.
I pause when others pause,
march to their step.
                              There is nothing
in our movements to distinguish us,
a loose-knit brotherhood pretending fealty
yet all yearning to be first to cross.

Cubism & Picasso

> On the wall, tightly imprisoned by right angles,
> the painting commands attention.
> Shapely arms clasp a patchwork
> of incomplete clues and incoherent images,
> splintered perspectives working voraciously
> to lay bare the imperfection of the world we live in;
> fragmented, obscure and discrete shards become whole,
> the unveiling of clues for ticking off a checklist.

Endowed with courage and vision,
 driven by obsession and dedication,
  such qualities tainted relationships
   and over-worked them to a muddy ochre.
    Life at the circus, death at the bullfights,
     and Art, the only things he was interested in;
      and Art, the only thing he was;
       and Art, the only thing.

> Greatness reveres the ones who commit to the process,
> who offer in two dimensions an illusion of depth,
> the ability to renew the world constantly
> and embody the inflection points
> in our culture.

Civilisations collide in unbounded curiosity / revitalised by brushstrokes, puffs of / colours merging on a gritty canvas. / Immersed in the clutter of exuberant minds / we focus inward to access our feelings, / to reassemble from their vision / our understanding of a shattered world.

Diagnosis

'There is a lump' he says, as if it's new.
There is a tone in this sudden-old voice
he's finally trying out,
a tone like a baby's inconsolable wailing,
a blend of anger and bemused disbelief
as if it's all someone else's fault.
It has been skulking in the shadows forever,
nurtured unknowingly across the years,
fed with worry, watered with failed schemes.
'I'm no gardener' he said once,
confused by a scrub of burnt lawn,
wilted phlox, horsetail run amok.
Soon they will christen it, as if giving it a name
makes it more personal, one of the family.
They will tell him that nothing is coincident;
the pain, the inability to hold fast to weight
or hit double-top like he used to.
'All these were signs' they'll say
- but he never paid any heed to signs.

His voice echoes on the telephone
as footsteps might a stone corridor,
betraying hollowness and emptiness
rather than the dull thud of a hostile invader.

LASTS

A Cracked Voice

a cracked voice
tries to recapture the glories of the past;
a fractured timbre more full
of passion
and understanding
than ever it was.

between fraying notes
fragmented by a now too-narrow range,
listen for the rhythm
rattling across the slippery silvery surface
like a skimming stone
we would suddenly have skip forever.

there.
everything you would seek is just there.
more than a shallow rattle-bag,
a mirror of unfathomable
and never-ending
depth.

Passion

where did it go
slipping like rainwater through
cracks   in   the   pavement
a deluge lost
fated to remain nothing   but a memory
a tale to be retold over tea and scones
as if we were just old friends
catching up
not people who were once
        caught out
                by the rain

Waves are not water

we are as waves are
>dissembling, pretending
>>to be something we are not
>>>misleading those who believe in form.
>>water is our Houdini-shape
>magic'd by science
rabbit-hatted,
>while we, energised by sleight of hand,
>>disguised and process-secret,
>>>pursue rude little exchanges
>>sustenance for the journey.
>ours is an unenviable pilgrimage
whose end we deny
>by pointing to glitzy sideshows,
>>lauding falsehood,
>>>seduced by the beauty
>>of a whale's spume as if
>surface breaking's what really matters.
the shore will come soon enough
>to fracture us noisily
>>to dissipate us in the shallow chaos
>>>when all that we were
>>abandons ship and
>we are no more than
an absence betrayed
>by loose shingle's shifting
>>and the whimper
>>>of a ripple.

When floating turned to drowning

We occupy the margins without thinking
trusting the water's meniscus
lying still and confident
the sun beating down.

Shocked by a tsunami invisibly small,
perception beyond all sensors
pricks at our peace
like a rogue white cloud
eye-line floating

or a shiver come from nowhere.

When did it happen
that floating turned to drowning?

Anthropology

you can smell things in the fog

even by the sea
ocean swells heaving against kelp-covered rocks
you sense - though not through sight or sound - a presence

it is the same everywhere

using only binoculars and a notebook
- as if either were of value! -
you are entranced by the prospect of discovering
a lost city whose impossibility is enticing
the colony you conjure has the promise of quiet industry
and beyond the mask of sea   sound   and fog
their undisturbed islands escaped looters' attention
chunks of marble from the ruins of ancient buildings
glimpsed through a small door in a gilded sculpture

in the fog you mis-hear the plainsong
of those robbed of devotion
a nocturne stolen from distant neighbours
carries the poignant voice of vulnerability
of finding only a provisionally happy ending
to a long sad story
                          or vice versa

The Cut-out

I try and imagine the irregular space he will leave,
the awkwardness of it. Will it have boundaries,
soft-boiled edges prone to compromise if you're careless,
like stranger-bumping in a Tesco's chiller aisle?
Stolen from unconcerned history and devoid of value,
I could take this abstract replica in all its coarse dimensions
and prop it tottering where he stood
to see if he's still at home in 'The Oak', the bookmakers,
the empty chair in the lethargic hospital waiting room.

It would be a validation of sorts.

I try and imagine the untrammelled space I will leave,
fluid and deep-sea'd, nebulous and shape-shifting.
Yet perhaps that's not how others remember us
preferring to recall the solid and tangible
something to be rebuked, or stroked, or prodded, or loved.
If you could take this insubstantial past-promise of me,
might you explore the sense of those rare few, to see
if contact with my roughly chiselled words
and hand-sewn pin-bled phrases touched them?

It could be a validation of sorts.

The Irresistible Fall

His was a mobile theatrical face
always primed for a cue from the wings.
Yet it was small too, mis-compiled,
victim of the boredom of growing-up.

Shaken by a sudden photograph,
I most recall a raucous laugh that challenged the world
as if all its scripts and tricks and fancies
could never be enough to derail him.

That it did was no surprise.
In the end he was undone by addiction
and a naivety that never left him,
his childishness both a blessing and a curse.

Gladys

You could have built walls from her dense cakes,
carved them into precisely defined slabs;
they were large, chocolatey and oddly grey
with the pitted consistency of breeze block.
Cutting the first slice after tea was a ritual,
a special treat for post-school Mondays.

In a house of twisted personalities
exaggerated by the mental shrapnel of war,
her laugh was resistant to misery and disease,
a cackle that challenged you to defy it,
exploding to deafen the under-breath chunter
of a brother who'd lost more than weight in Burma.

I felt for Uncle George, marooned like me,
as long-suffering as he was grey-topped tall,
handcuffed to a recurrent Poe-like nightmare
from which he could never escape -
or from which she would never release him.
I was too young then to decipher life.

One by one, death smuggled them away,
though only after I had been partially rescued.
Arthur's going finally ended his bitter war,
and not even her laugh could save George,
silently eaten away from the inside
all the while defending his back-bent dignity.

Suffering, punishment, and freedom
I discovered later; a three-card-trick
played chest-close, queen hidden up the sleeve.

In a theatre beyond our vanquishing,
she rescued a child who loved her cakes
and who missed the chance to thank her.

Congregation at a Twitcher's Sunset

"They beat out rhythmic drum solos on hollow trees.
They watch me, watching them.
They watch me as spies would,
        always out of reach.

"Some bring gifts.
Gift-giving is their natural encore
        placing them where they can't be missed.
By my bed, a small wooden box,
        each compartment guarding treasure:
        a gold bead, a pearl earring,
        a quartz crystal, a red Lego brick."

He comes to understand the purpose of meaningful sounds,
        understands a culture of tool-making is important,
        that complicated societies are the real spur
        for making informed decisions.
All too late, he discovers
        an uncanny ability to distinguish expressions,
        the alphabet, paintings by Monet and Picasso.

He yearns for his home and treasures
        during an illness long and drawn out.
Hard-wiring underlies memory and decision-making;
        his own is flawed, fraying, fragile.

They watch him as spies would,
        already decked out in their mourning dress.

Early Edition

They stand on the pavement
>   waiting.

Up before everyone, larks and all,
they stroll down the road ever slower,
struggling not to beat the first bus from the depot
- and failing because they must get out.

Today they are too early
>   again.

Unlocking a grill-protected door
paint-flaked from too many winters,
Ray nods with a yawn
acknowledging their vigil,
silent knights, avoiding eye contact,
as if hiding ancient secrets from each other.
Inside, on the counter,
'The Mail', two copies of 'The Sun',
one 'Telegraph', ready and waiting -
and a space where there used to be an 'Express'
until old Bob left them.

Moments later
what might pass for a rush is over.
Ray returns to his tea.

Nodding farewell to each other,
the Mail, the Suns and the Telegraph
make their separate ways
back to the echo of empty houses

on the edge of the estate;
off to replay their cycle of memories
and waiting.
Tomorrow they will beat the alarm again
- please God -
and shuffle down the road
for the newspaper that signals
another day survived.

Inheritance

Above the silent still of an evergreen canopy
a spire of smoke rises lazy into summer dusk.
Unhurried like the thin grey column,
settlers prepare for an enemy attack
confident in their organisation and discipline,
hopeful there is strength in numbers.
Worn down by the poverty of living too long
on a boomerang of arid sand,
theirs had been a weary pilgrimage
sustained by the promise of green.

An unrequited search spawns speculation as
whispering academics misread a fading scroll
lying naked on a light-table,
trying to expose the secrets
of a past it was meant to protect.

Outside, in a chill corridor, she waits
professing to be a descendant, the last remaining,
desperate for her claim to be legitimised.

Changing Trains

An express lances through a verdant cutting.
Insistent, a tell-tale whistle of air
against an aerodynamic shell,
forced aside as the train
has somewhere more important to be.
The tuning-fork wheel hum
on unending miles of extruded track
robs us of a heartbeat,
like grieving for that throat-clearing cough
from the first few puffs of steam.

Our past was once green-flagged,
waived from when doors were click-slammed
and heads were thrust through lowered windows -
then thrust back in at sudden tunnels,
our reflex to be dark-scared,
the dank and dripping arcing walls
feared closer than they could have been.

A compulsion to change trains
seeds itself like growing-up,
a sacrifice of the leisurely and romantic
for the functional's vacuous promise,
as if getting somewhere faster was all that mattered.

Accompanied by its uniform sound
our modern plastic train takes us
away from the yearned for:
the romance of waiting with a notebook,
a pencil, a curled ham sandwich.
It takes us away from a station once

crafted of delicately wrought ironwork,
pilasters of sculpted marble.
There is no discovery now. Nothing more
than a jumble of signs in a modern font,
fast food, noise and litter; an antiseptic terminal
devoid of character and satisfaction.

We could be anywhere.

And nowhere.

Did we know those days were golden?

There is bravado in our voices
when we talk about the past,
recall episodes as jewels
inherited from a celebrated ancestor,
pretend we had known all along
they were sparkling points of learning
not moments lost to the breeze
like insignificant dandelion seed.
We smuggle away regret, keep it hidden
like an embarrassing Aunt
who constantly knits unshapely things,
murmuring and click-clacking her needles
while we feign not to notice the impact
of a persistent lack of personal hygiene.

Perhaps we might have marked it back then,
the incremental decay that stalked us,
invisible, defying recognition.
                                      We know it now.

And Somewhere in Between

Rumours of a breakthrough in the search for the meaning of life

there were scattered news reports
        crackling through on ancient valve radios
that a microscope for living had been forged
        from a century of accumulated science

vexed by uncertainties in theories
        loosened like frayed strands of a DNA tapestry
one has never stopped weaving
        we look back for missed opportunities
hopelessly mining inaccurate data
        on the metrics of human activity
to try and prove there could have been
        alternative outcomes under different scenarios

the curse of old age is to be blessed with
        a blend of urgency and wisdom
to be wary of the harlot of understanding
        to be mired in the close-up   knowing that
every day is another in a turbulent transition
        the resisting of admonitions to grow up

Harvesting

a pitchfork stab crudely
pierces the word-stack
inadequate implement
in the search for a needle
a glitter-glimmer in the pale kaleidoscope
of straw confusion

hollow-light fragments fuse
and ally their strength
their weight together
brutally heavy
threatening fracture
of the elegant tines

blister-bringing effort defies description
on the pilgrimage to relief
contortion   anguish
seem inappropriate
then the load shifted
able to breathe out again

here comes the baler
to secure wind-teased morsels
made inflexible
and all for ease
the readiness to be shelved
indistinguishable   forgotten

undiminished
the fork seeks out
the next unruly stack

Gas Street Basin

Forty years   misplaced.
Brushed aside
    like Stuart's glasses branch-snagged
    casually flipped slow-motion
    into canal-dark water at the last-morning tiller
    between here and somewhere else.

Years dissolving   inexplicably
as a gentle wake
    resolves back into nothing but a ripple
    the tried and tested ruse
    of leaving not a trace of our recent passing
    for the silent boats that follow.

In harsh shadows   ghostly
memories dance;
    memories of mooring ropes and narrow bunks
    and pubs now driven from soft focus
    into something they didn't used to be
    trapped in their own navigation.

Barley wine.   Skittles.
Courses charted.
    Uncertain fragments wistfully recalled
    as the unexpected bequest of an unplanned stroll,
    spectres on the Gas Street towpath
    after all these rapidly accelerating years.

Deauville

A pristine boardwalk of uniform treads
stretches deceptively across the sand,
past cafes and restaurants too expensive
and too French for the provincial Anglo.
Menus, dressed in the most expensive fonts,
boast elegance and complexity at a sophisticated price
as if no-one might casually want
just a coffee or a coke and a sit-down.
Hard on our heels alienation gallops
teasing us for our cheap t-shirts and shorts,
mocking the way we attempt to stroll
bereft of any sang froid or je ne c'est quoi.

Self-conscious, we are chased away
and escape along the coastal roads
relieved to find Honfleur more inclusive;
the quaint little harbour, recognisable rustic rolls
laced with ham, perfect for tourists.
Breathing out again, it is a place that saves the day.

Years later, is this all that is remembered,
displacement, discomfort, relief?

That
        and sitting at too small a restaurant table,
        five of us in a space for three,
        elbows knocking as we galloped through lunch.
That
        and later, back at the remote cottage
        riding rusty old bikes, watching cows in the field,
        praising Eddy's rudimentary portraits.

That
        and the sight of your blistered feet
        because I had insisted no-one in France
        wore socks with sandals.

On the verge of new love

This is a rare visitor, this trembling,
though I have never been one to willingly submit to
                                                    'palpitations'
      of any sort.

Questions are begged   such as
how can your own room seem foreign territory
and give you that tipping-point feeling
       the thrill of the unexpected   or the unknown
            the anticipation of a child?

But look at us now.
            As far from childhood
as it is possible to be.
                    Well, almost.

Attachment

The house her parents left her was too large,
        the car too old.
To compensate, she filled the house with friends,
        and drove never-ending miles.
To both she gave names,
        'Henry' suiting the car.
Now I wonder if they had been
        her only true friends.

I lived our brief relationship
        as if continually redrafting a poem,
ideals, words and an a blurred self-image
        always between us.
I had wanted the beauty of rhyming couplets
        not seeing she lived her life
as if it were experimental free verse
        strangely staccato;
there was little place for soft edges,
        the ludicrously romantic.

Should it have been a surprise she ended up
        calling Rome her home,
giving parties in a villa's catacombs,
        and living as she always had,
erecting barriers to protect her
        from too much affection?

Modern Warfare

Spending their young lives working   in the trenches
they grew up culturally confused,   ending up
searching for a purpose   a connection,
distancing themselves   from belief
in favour of an education   and the promise of a better future.

Seamlessly switching from slang   to jokes   to quotes
he became a spokesman despite forebodings,   wanting
to reclaim a culture   stripped from people,
seeking colour and flavour   in old mosaics
and translating faith into a lingo   more common than pizza.

        The antidote to apathy uselessly picks
        at a new digital lock on the door;
        a phone call in the dead of night confirming
        that being human has become more difficult.

20/20

They see their town slipping into decline;
the hospital on the brink of bankruptcy,
a shopping mall closing.
Not renowned for metaphors,
economists are recording 'deaths of despair'.

Confronting the erosion of their majority status
is an unresolvable problem for people
who built something from the ground up,
who yearn for a repeat of their treasured history
like a cable re-run of a forties' black-and-white movie.

Vulnerable, wowed by the theatrical,
they succumb to mirrors and smoking dry-ice,
to polo shirts and khakis stepping out of the shadows -
the neighbourhood normal, gun-toting from the saddle
of a re-sprayed carousel stallion.

To protect themselves from a lack of bias,
these new veterans cite research that distills
their problem into a few vacuous words
which they bow-wrap and hand out,
the illusion of gifting something tangible.

The peril of language is our weakness,
as potent as shaking a fist at a thunder cloud.
And all the while the soundbite marches on,
stories spiral forward propelled by their own weight,
and sanity dances towards the edge of the precipice.

ex-Curricula

Framed by the backdrop of a graffiti-covered wall
they are animated by civic and political urgency
feeling their safety and humanity under siege.

They seek the freedom to convene beyond classrooms,
juggling joy and vehemence in equal degree
wanting to disrupt the way things are.

Learning how to be brave demands the courage
to unfurl parts of themselves
and the testing of their values.

Theirs is a perennial yet nascent enquiry;
trying to measure progress is naive,
like looking for a sun resting between yesterday and today.

[* partly inspired by the 2018 protests against gun laws following multiple shootings at US schools.]

Ganglands = Politics

Fine tuning our mental radar
- the constant fingering of the dial in ever-smaller increments -
we watch fluctuating shadows for ambushes,
violent attacks over semi-precious resources
undertaken at randomly selected moments.
Fear awakens our tribal minds
to connect us to group identities;
individuality and empathy vanish,
masked by the gang's resplendent tattoo.

If you could strip away this veneer of belonging
you might witness collaboration between former activists
helping each other side-step barely disguised traps
to focus solely on a common objective.

At ease again, they might once more embrace
: the power of language.

Threat

Camouflaged by the city, men on mopeds
sheathed in helmets and the immature roar of under-powered engines,
>	keep their dialogue to themselves.

With little idea we are being watched
there is no vulnerability,
>	no fear that we are profoundly exposed.

Somewhere strangers measure us through lenses never seen,
our casual movements recorded
>	and analysed in endless tabulations.

Privacy is a commodity for those with serious money;
public safety the pretext for surveillance.
>	Welcome to the daily cadence of the Earth.

DNA

Scavenged from dusty boxes in mixed auction lots
or freed from faded albums, warped gilt frames,
the pockets of frayed and ruined uniforms,
old photos are handed down long past the point
where their images are verifiable.
They are snapshots of memory seeking
their place in some vaguely determined hierarchy.

A photograph. The instant when the shutter opens:
one sixtieth,

              one hundredth,

                            one fragment of time.

The subjects just so, staring this way or that,
time-locked by a hat, a coat, the background livery.
Perhaps they frown, concerned at the weather,
smile on demand, or at a scene
just witnessed from the corner of their eye.
And the unseen hand holding the camera?
It is impossible to say.

Back then, the naked eye was the primary tool
to rationalise the truth of what they saw.

Faced with too much data to handle,
those charged with building the Catalogue
were compromised by superficial combinations.
So they developed a science to suit their prejudices,
setting aside the mal-aligned,
driving discrimination and displacement
in pursuit of the purity of the image.

They embraced crude and coarse categories,
gave names to the tangible,
names that fit into their schema of self and supremacy
- like Morton's skulls and Nazi ideals.

Years later, inevitably unable to re-locate groups
geographically dispersed at best,
we return to the security of mythology
and to those slivers of time cast adrift, abandoned, unowned.
When the people who are the links have gone
what is left but a verbal narrative
and an obsession with stories
                                - the kind that families tell
when a tour of their past is a haunting experience?

Time eventually found ways to photograph the invisible,
sequences within sequences that make us what we are
- which in the end is not so very different,
the ultimate simplification of the family.

Reconstruction

Arriving as a stranger
he sees broad gleaming rivers everywhere,
steep patchwork valleys,
pastures spread like velveteen cloaks,
high rolling hills quilted in soft green folds.
Below, the remote town is crowded and graceless.

For a full week they hid,
seeing the black smoke coming and knowing what it meant.
After, assaulted by the sight of charred houses
and the lingering smell of death,
they became as incapable of optimism as of flight.

Reshaped by violence and decades of ideological warfare,
was it choice or lack of choice that prompted their return
to this most unlikely promised land?
They built a history lesson from their own experience
and taught it to hungry listeners in a room
barely large enough for a hermit.

Undercurrent

Just one more in an endless string of chores,
risking your life to protect others is part of the deal;
at the root of our evolutionary past,
empathy the kindling that fires compassion.

Interrogation by a person in a lab coat
is the price paid for significant advances
in the unravelling of the science behind selflessness:

"Under controlled conditions,
       cries of pain were recorded
then played back to our subjects
       to see if they could recognise any moral violation."

Sometimes one justifies the worst of actions
to preserve an illusion of humanity.

The Mirage of Progress

Trapped in the heat between mountain ranges
where the air is lip-chapping dry, Dust Devils spin,
harbinger winds blowing death from the sun-baked lake
salt-coating farms whose barren tracts kiss the horizon.

Loosed from the deep recesses of time, an arid
iron-rich landscape unfurls like a leaf-shaped bowl.
Beyond recognition, the gentle incline of the old lake shore;
and there, a fish skull bleached brilliant white,
      a discarded pair of rubber boots,
            boats abandoned in cracked silt,
                  piers that lead to nowhere.

In a flash of evaporation
turquoise waters mineral-stained blood-red,
their legacy, a photo opportunity for the intrepid
unencumbered with a sense of how it once was.

Global Warning

Shallow pools of meltwater reflect high summer sun
in the empty immensity glazing the top of our world.

Winds and currents conspire
 to generate   imperceptible   drifts,
  journeys   that   will   last   years.

And as the ice erode s
development intrudes -
a trend accelerates
new figures arriving in a sterile landscape
beginning to blaze with life.

Species are thrust into closer contact;
nearby evidence of a kill,
a scarlet highlight
palette-
       knife-
              spread
                      on the snow-covered sea.

The guide and advisor to our expedition,
no longer at home in his shrinking world, says

"This is not a linear story where we know how it ends".

Peasant Farming

In a valley ringed by dusky mountains,
in a rhythm that continues for hours,
wiry figures with rutted tawny skin
ploughed from years of labouring
plunge home home-made pitchforks to free
emerald-hued plants bound for the city.

They distrust machines that till the land,
eating boiled bark when the food runs out;
they hang laundry in the backyards
of houses arrayed in weary clutches
that dead-end in spent cornfields and
smells that seldom achieve the pleasant.

Here, life embodies a kind of time travel:
ideology, tradition, and response.

The Hopeless Wager

It was, they said, a cinch,
though I, suspicious of all 'good-things'
reserved the right to disbelieve,
a prerogative to be sceptical.
Or, misunderstanding perhaps, was it no more
than a statement of fact,
a pointing to equestrian tack,
fallible hardware to keep the rider onboard?

Later, after mounting loses
(appreciate the play on words, please!)
I uncovered an ancient card game
where the five of trumps
- the most powerful card there is -
is also called the cinch.

Perhaps nothing is certain
after all.
Perhaps there are no 'sure things'
- no cinches.
Or almost none.

Telling the time

I read words not stencilled on the sign,
interpreting a hidden meaning.
Mallet-hammered, pine-posted,
the laminated message
stapled to a plywood square
occupies the same space as before:
the grass verge just as you breast
the crown of the hill.
Mundane enough, its words
surreal rather than cryptic,
beg to be taken literally:
'Annual Duck Race, Bank Hol. Mon.'.
Appropriately sponsor-tagged
and removed from their natural habitat,
the ducks -
yellow
plastic
uniform
- bob on the canal,
tossed in and wind-blown
to some imaginary winning line.
Obtusely, I think of how
plastic *can* be recycled
and how the sign really reads
"That's another year gone then".

The Thief

The Thief comes in silence,
in slumber-deep darkness,
creeping through window-cracked night,
leaving no fingerprints.

The Thief comes in daylight
just as your back is turned,
when you are sense-distracted,
attention poor.

Nervous on a sudden whim
you feel your pocket for a wallet,
search your wrist for a watch
or last Christmas' present.

You pause for a ghost,
a sound misplaced, out of context:
the gravel-tell of footsteps,
the whisper of a breath.

A grave-trod shiver
forces a halting laugh-out-loud,
a hope you were unobserved
thrown by the irrational.

Yet what can the Thief steal
apart from your peace of mind,
slivers of your dignity,
another morsel of your time?

untitled haiku

a few precious words
are released unprotected
into the maelstrom

living on their wits
and the genius to melt
into an image

trick of the mind's eye
to trace pattern myth and ghosts
in the never-there

when we caress them
our crass manipulation
falls so often short

yet there they remain
imperious and perfect
our slaves and masters

The Myth of You

look for an inauspicious door
left hand-width ajar
and push
gently
do not knock
gauge with that sixth sense
you never knew you had
the potential of the space
beyond
weigh its dimensions
draft the atmosphere
in charcoal
dark
and finger-smudged
sketch the tension
air-clashed
by the bow-wave of your coming
your intrusion
replaces the unseen
frees the unfelt
an exchange of sorts
while the myth of you
remains outside

Fossil-hunting

We travel down a gravel road to a broken bank
dust kicking up from the skidding tyres
as they struggle for grip on a misjudged incline.

The backdrop is a panoply of greys.
Above the rough sea, the clouds push hard towards us,
White Horses fling their manes to the cold-washed beach.
The whistle of the wind, the crash of the waves,
a symphonic backing for the rough snarl
of the gravel-spewing tyres.

Imprinted in the scattered stone, slight
after-images of an intricate shadow thrown decades ago.

Imagine a forest, late-day sun
slanting through unfamiliar foliage;
the smell of the forest floor, perhaps pine,
the sweetness of recent-crushed leaves,
or the residue of fruits half-eaten by unseen beasts.
On a cold, grey, shingle beach
a stone tracing preserves that day,
the capture of an autumn afternoon.

Departing, imagine the wheel-spin
as we strive for grip on the broken bank,
our words disappearing, leaving no known descendants.

Acknowledgements

- My thanks to members of the North Yorkshire Stanza group. Early drafts of a small number of these poems were shared with my friends there, the inevitable consequence being that the versions contained in this book are undoubtedly more polished than when they first saw the light of day!
- The cover image is cut from a photo taken on 9th November, 1967, from the Earth-orbital Apollo 4 (Spacecraft 017/Saturn 501) space mission, and shows the Atlantic Ocean, Antarctica, looking west, as photographed. The spacecraft was orbiting Earth at an altitude of 8,628 miles at the time. The image was made available free of copyright and for general use at www.commons.wikimedia.org.

www.ingramcontent.com/pod-product-compliance
Lightning Source LLC
Chambersburg PA
CBHW030533080526
44586CB00011B/423